Wendy Moreno is married and is a mother to an amazing son. She is self-employed and runs a successful pet-sitting service. Wendy has combined her two passions in her children's books—cats and daydreaming.

Copyright © Wendy Moreno (2019)

All rights reserved. No part of this publication may be reproduced, distributed, or transmitted in any form or by any means, including photocopying, recording, or other electronic or mechanical methods, without the prior written permission of the publisher, except in the case of brief quotations embodied in critical reviews and certain other non-commercial uses permitted by copyright law. For permission requests, write to the publisher.

Any person who commits any unauthorized act in relation to this publication may be liable to criminal prosecution and civil claims for damages.

Ordering Information:
Quantity sales: special discounts are available on quantity purchases by corporations, associations, and others. For details, contact the publisher at the address below.

Publisher's Cataloging-in-Publication data

Moreno, Wendy
Murphy, Wake Up!

ISBN 9781643785714 (Paperback)
ISBN 9781643785721 (Hardback)
ISBN 9781645368199 (ePub e-book)

Library of Congress Control Number: 2019911785

The main category of the book — JUVENILE FICTION / Animals / Cats

www.austinmacauley.com/us

First Published (2019)
Austin Macauley Publishers LLC
40 Wall Street, 28th Floor
New York, NY 10005
USA
mail-usa@austinmacauley.com
+1 (646) 5125767

I dedicate this book to my wonderful son, Anthony, my amazing husband, Bob, and my fur-ever beloved kitty, Murphy.

Thank you, honey, for all your thoughts, ideas, love, and support.
This book could not have been created without you.

This is Murphy. Murphy is at it again.
He has his eye on the backpack.

"Hmm, this will do," says Murphy.
"Just right for a nice long nap."

"Zzz...Zzz...Zzz...Zzz...Zzz...Zzz..."

Murphy is at it again! He has found a place to sleep, but it is not his bed. It is the boy's backpack for school.

"This is nice.

PURR, PURR, PURR.

Zzz, Zzz, Zzz."

"Just the right place for me to leave a few fur balls."

"This is nice.

PURR, PURR, PURR.

Zzz, Zzz, Zzz."

DING DING DING!!!

It is time for school. Class is about to start.

"Hi, my name is Murphy. What is your name?"

"Hi, Murphy.
My name is Angel.
Will you be my friend?"

"Hello, Angel.
It is nice to meet you.
You will be my first school friend."

"I am hungry!
When is lunch?"
says Murphy.

The teacher asks the class to draw a picture of something they like.

"Murphy, what will you draw?" Angel asks.

"I think I will draw a playground. I like playgrounds." says Murphy

"Great!" says Angel. "What can I draw for your playground? I know. I will draw some pretty flowers. They will smell good."

No flowers! NO FLOWERS! Flowers will not be in my playground."

"I want my picture to go with yours.
Flowers will be so pretty, and they smell good too!"
Angel smiles.

"There will only be a swing...

a great big slide...

And lots of bars to climb on.

"Please, Murphy. Flowers will make your playground so pretty, and they smell good too."

"OKAY! OKAY! OKAY!

"Yes, you can draw flowers for my playground. But not too many and I do not want to smell them either."

"Is it lunchtime yet? I am hungry! I want fries!"

"Murphy, wake up! That is my backpack for school. You are getting fur all over it."

"Phew... Flowers?

"Flowers do not belong in playgrounds. Only swings, slides, and bars."

"Hmm... Where can I get some sleep? Where can I go? I know...

"On to my next spot!"

CPSIA information can be obtained
at www.ICGtesting.com
Printed in the USA
BVHW020831210920
589269BV00017B/423